Masters of Music

THE WORLD'S GREATEST COMPOSERS

The Life and Times of

Scott Joplin

Mitchell Lane PUBLISHERS

P.O. Box 196
Hockessin, Delaware 19707

Masters of Music
THE WORLD'S GREATEST COMPOSERS

Titles in the Series
The Life and Times of...

Visit us on the web: www.mitchelllane.com
Comments? email us: mitchelllane@mitchelllane.com

Masters of Music

THE WORLD'S GREATEST COMPOSERS

The Life and Times of

Scott Joplin

by John Bankston

Mitchell Lane
PUBLISHERS

Printing   3   4   5   6   7   8
     Library of Congress Cataloging-in-Publication Data
Bankston, John, 1974-
    The life and times of Scott Joplin / John Bankston.
        p. cm. — (Masters of music. The world's greatest composers)
    Includes bibliographical references (p.   ) and index.
    Contents: Son of a slave—The struggle after the freedom—The piano man—Turning over a new leaf—Ragtime opera.
    ISBN 1-58415-270-2 (library bound)
    1. Joplin, Scott, 1868-1917—Juvenile literature. 2. Composers—United States—Biography—Juvenile literature. [1. Joplin, Scott, 1868-1917. 2. Composers. 3. African Americans—Biography.] I. Title. II. Masters of music. World's greatest composers.
ML3930.J66B35 2004
780'.92—dc22

                                                              2003024334

ISBN 13: 9781584152484

ABOUT THE AUTHOR: Born in Boston, Massachussetts, **John Bankston** began publishing articles in newspapers and magazines while still a teenager. Since then, he has written over two hundred articles, and contributed chapters to books such as *Crimes of Passion*, and *Death Row 2000*, which have been sold in bookstores across the world. He has written numerous biographies for young adults, including *The Life and Times of Wolfgang Amadeus Mozart* and *Randolph Caldecott and the Story of the Caldecott Medal* (Mitchell Lane). He currently lives in Portland, Oregon.

PUBLISHER'S NOTE: This story is based on the author's extensive research, which he believes to be accurate. Documentation of such research is contained on page 47.

The internet sites referenced herein were active as of the publication date. Due to the fleeting nature of some web sites, we cannot guarantee they will all be active when you are reading this book.

Contents

The Life and Times of
Scott Joplin

by John Bankston

* For Your Information

In the 1800s, the most popular form of entertainment was playing the piano or guitar, with the rest of the family or guests singing along. Sheet music sales were as important then as album sales are today.

Son of a Slave

The boy began to dance. He was a small child, and he seemed controlled by an invisible puppet master as he wiggled and shook his limbs. He wasn't, of course. Instead, the bouncing notes coming from a nearby piano were insisting that he move.

How could he not? The man behind the piano was playing a rhythm that made it impossible to sit still. It wasn't gospel music, it wasn't a march, and it surely wasn't classical. It was ragtime, and already it seemed to have an entire nation tapping its collective feet.

The pianist was Scott Joplin. He'd been trying to sell one of his "rags" without success. So he decided on a gimmick. Surely the dancing boy would convince a music publisher of the composition's power.

The music publisher's name was John Stark. He owned a small company in the town of Sedalia, Missouri. If he liked a song, he bought the sheet music and had copies made of it. Then he sold the copies to people who played the songs at their own pianos.

The year was 1899. At that time, music wasn't recorded. It was sold as sheet music. A talented writer could earn a decent living composing popular songs for other people to play. That was what Scott Joplin was hoping for.

He was now in his early thirties. He'd spent years playing the piano in smoke-filled bars and riding the rails for music tours. He earned extra money giving piano lessons, but what he really wanted to be was a full-time composer. Would this finally be his chance?

When he stopped playing, the boy stopped dancing, and for a moment there was silence.

Then publisher John Stark told pianist Scott Joplin the words he'd been waiting to hear. They had a deal. The song was "Maple Leaf Rag." It got its name from the saloon where it was first played, a club over a feed store in downtown Sedalia.

Scott would soon make the club, and ragtime music, famous. Although other composers had already written ragtime compositions, Scott's would be the first to sell over one million copies. His work was part of the reason ragtime remained popular for the next two decades. Today the rhythms of ragtime can be heard in jazz, the blues, and rock and roll. Scott Joplin altered existing songs in the same way that hip-hop and techno artists would do a century later.

Scott was the son of a former slave. Some of the first musical notes he heard had been handed down from the plantation. Slaves from Africa brought their own native music with them and then combined it with the hymns and spirituals they learned in the United States. They sang the songs in the fields and performed them for their owners in the plantation homes. It was music that came from bondage and only began to reach a wider audience following their freedom.

Publisher John Stark bought Joplin's "Maple Leaf Rag" in 1899. The two of them remained in business together for more than 10 years.

Scott memorized the music he learned as a child and combined it with the popular tunes of his time. The world of slavery had been vividly described to white people in the early 1850s in the novel *Uncle Tom's Cabin*. The music of the slaves would reach the same audience first through the stereotypical minstrel shows of the 1870s, then through the compositions of men like Scott Joplin.

Scott was a member of the first generation of African Americans in the United States who were born after the end of slavery. He was a man of contradictions, a classically trained pianist who spent several years playing in saloons. His work cut across geography, race, class, and time. He was in every way a Master of Music. ◆

Stowe's Uncle Tom's Cabin *was made into a movie at least eleven times. These scenes from Harry A. Pollard's 1927 version show slaves before (top) and after (bottom) emancipation.*

Uncle Tom's Cabin FYInfo

During the time Scott Joplin's father was a slave, a woman named Harriet Beecher Stowe was making her voice heard against slavery. The daughter of a famous Congregational minister, Stowe had been a successful writer for years when the issue compelled her to write her most famous book.

Born in Connecticut, she spent her early adult life in Cincinnati, Ohio, where her husband was a college professor. The city was filled with escaped slaves trying to make it north to Canada and freedom. Stowe learned that her own maid, who'd claimed to be a freewoman,

Harriet Beecher Stowe

was actually an escaped slave. According to the law, Stowe should have turned the maid in. Instead she and her husband helped the woman flee to Canada.

The Fugitive Slave Act of 1850 allowed southern slave owners to enter free states like Ohio to capture escaped slaves. The law enraged many northerners, who saw it as accepting slavery in states where it was illegal. Stowe's feelings about the issue were cemented by a trip to Kentucky when she witnessed a slave's abuse by an owner. The image haunted her for years.

"I feel now that the time is come when even a woman or a child who can speak a word for freedom and humanity is bound to speak," Stowe said in a letter to Dr. Gamaliel Bailey, the owner of an antislavery newspaper.[1] She had written a book about slavery based on her experiences and reliable reports from people she knew. Although fictional, its depiction was very realistic for the times.

Bailey agreed to publish the book in a series in his newspaper. Called *Uncle Tom's Cabin*, the first installment appeared on June 5, 1851. The series was very popular. The popularity continued when the installments were published as a book a year later. *Uncle Tom's Cabin* made Stowe famous. It also made many northerners rethink their feelings about the slavery issue, an important step toward eventually eliminating it. Some historians believe that the book was one of the causes of the Civil War.

Harriet Beecher Stowe

Abraham Lincoln (right) signed the Emancipation Proclamation, which granted slaves their freedom, in 1863.

The Struggle After the Freedom

Giles Joplin's life began with the stroke of a pen. It was probably sometime in 1859 or 1860, just before the Civil War would tear the United States apart. Giles's former home state of South Carolina was the first to secede from— or leave—the United States in December 1860. Four months later, Confederate soldiers attacked South Carolina's Fort Sumter, and the Civil War officially began.

The Civil War was fought for many reasons, but a major one was over people like Giles Joplin. Giles, an African American, was born a slave. That meant he had no rights. He was looked at as property, like a horse or a mule, although many plantation owners treated their animals better than their slaves.

Giles was fortunate. His master granted him his freedom several years before President Abraham Lincoln signed the Emancipation Proclamation on January 1, 1863, and officially ended bondage for millions of slaves. Giles was almost certainly living in Texas at the time of his release. There is a census record in 1850 of a slave named "Jiles" (a spelling that is also commonly used) who had arrived in the northeast corner of Texas from South Carolina a few months earlier at the age of eight. Eventually Giles became the property of a man named Josiah Joplin and took the same last name. Soon afterward, he was granted his freedom. As a slave he'd been a musician, playing the violin at the plantation's "big house," but as a free man his wages came from hard labor.

It didn't take long for him to meet Florence Givens, who'd grown up free in Texas after her family moved from Kentucky. She worked for the church he attended. They dated briefly before marrying.

The couple lived at a time when there were far fewer records than there are now, especially for African Americans. There were no hospital admissions, no birth certificates. Their first son, Monroe, probably was born at about the same time that Fort Sumter came under attack. Many accounts say that their second son, Scott, was born on November 24, 1868, in Bowie, a county in northeastern Texas. Robert followed a year later, and a girl, Ossie, came a year after Robert. Willie and Myrtle would eventually round out the family.

For a while, Giles worked as a sharecropper—farming and living on land owned by someone else. It was almost as bad as slavery. The family lived in several different places, and Giles had trouble keeping his family fed. When he learned that the Texas and Pacific Railroad was hiring laborers in Texarkana, he decided to move there.

Texarkana was a rapidly growing town on the border between Texas and Arkansas about thirty miles north of Louisiana. Its name came from a combination of the three states: TEX-as, ARK-ansas, and Louisi-ANA. Most African Americans settled on the Arkansas side, which was less expensive The whites lived on the more well-to-do Texas side. There was also a small African-American section in Texas, and Giles Joplin settled his family there in 1875.

As writer James Haskins notes, "For young Scott Joplin, Texarkana was an exciting place to be. The sandy hills and spring mudholes presented numerous opportunities for play, and the town was abustle with continuous activity. Here land was being cleared, there new frame houses were being erected, often to replace earlier structures that had been destroyed by fire. Tinderbox-like, the town buildings frequently burned, and it was exciting to watch the townspeople form bucket brigades and pass buckets of water to throw on the fire. Perhaps, like most young boys, Scott also looked forward to being part of the bucket brigade, as his father frequently was."[1]

Whether or not Scott ever joined the bucket brigade is just one of the many mysteries of his life. There will always be some question about many dates and events in any story of Scott Joplin. But one thing is certain. His early talent is undeniable. He grew up in a musical family. Besides his father's skill with the violin, his mother played the banjo and sang. For some reason Monroe didn't develop musically, but the other boys did, playing the banjo, the guitar, and the violin. The two girls would become professional singers. The Joplin family could have formed their own band if they had wanted to.

Before fire departments became established throughout the country, people would form bucket brigades to put out fires. Scott Joplin's father was often part of bucket brigades in Texarkana, where the houses were mostly made of wood and burned easily.

Scott tried the same instruments as his brothers and even played bugle with a local band. Scott's father introduced him to classical music, and his mother took him to church where the gospel melodies seemed to fill him like a starving man at a buffet.

Soon after their arrival in Texarkana, Scott's mother took him with her on a cleaning job. Inside the house of a wealthy lawyer named W. G. Cook, the seven-year-old boy discovered a beautiful piano.

At church he'd seen an organ played, and he was probably familiar with piano music. But he'd never touched one before. It was like a perfectly, brand-new toy. No one else was around. He begged his mother to let him try it.

She gave him permission. Scott sat in front of the instrument and soon was banging out an imperfect little melody. He'd never had a lesson, but Florence could tell he had a gift.

His mother scraped together enough money to pay a local man named J. C. Johnson to give lessons to Scott. Johnson was multi-racial and multi-talented, doing everything from running a barber shop to selling real estate. It didn't take him long to see Scott was the real thing. When Florence didn't have enough money to keep paying for lessons, the man kids nicknamed "The Professor" started teaching Scott for free.

As a boy, Scott was similar to Wolfgang Amadeus Mozart, the Austrian composer who'd grown up a century before. Both picked up music early, demonstrating an ability to play by ear—playing without needing to read notes. Like Mozart, Scott began playing several instruments as a child before settling on the piano by the time he was eight. In a way, Scott was fortunate. Mozart spent his childhood touring Europe and perhaps becoming famous too soon, while Scott's talent grew quietly in Texarkana beneath his parents' watchful eyes.

Like Scott Joplin, Wolfgang Amadeus Mozart, pictured here, was also a child prodigy on the piano.

When Johnson wasn't able to keep teaching him, Scott was lucky enough to meet Julius Weiss. He was a German immigrant who made a living tutoring the children of the wealthier families in Texarkana. Like the Professor, Weiss quickly recognized Scott's talent. Also like the Professor, Weiss taught the boy for free. He gave Scott a firm grounding in classical piano technique. By the time Scott was twelve, he could compose his own music and improvise, or make up songs as he played.

It seems Scott learned so quickly and practiced so often, the lessons were soon unnecessary. He may not have needed them, but he sorely needed an instrument. In middle-class homes in the late nineteenth century, a piano was as common as a CD player is today. Scott's parents weren't middle class, they were struggling, but somehow they managed to find him a decent secondhand piano.

Scott rarely had to be asked to practice, but as he approached his teens, Giles was worried. He was afraid his son loved music *too* much. Music should be a hobby, not a career, he thought. He knew how tough life as an African American in post-Civil War America could be. Scott would only make it harder by hanging his future on some crazy dream.

While Scott was growing up, the country had entered into a period of enormous challenges. The wounds created by the Civil War took far longer to heal than the conflict itself. The period of

Reconstruction saw northerners and Union soldiers overseeing the South, enforcing the new amendments to the U.S. Constitution: the Thirteenth which outlawed slavery, the Fourteenth which gave citizenship to former slaves, and the Fifteenth which gave them the right to vote—the men, that is. American women of any race would have to wait until 1920 before they could vote.

As a result, men who'd been slaves just a decade earlier were now able to vote. A few African Americans actually won elections. Still, many African Americans were poorly treated, and they suffered from the aftereffects of slavery. Most freed slaves were illiterate—they couldn't read or write, and they had few job skills. For the first time, they had to deal with the normal day-to-day challenges of finding a job and taking care of a home. It was far better than slavery, of course, but many fell into a time of poverty.

The United States fared better than most countries do after a civil war, where peace is short-lived and violent conflicts continue for years. Still, for many African Americans, violence remained a grim reality. The year Scott was born, whites killed nearly 400 freedmen in Texas. Two years previously, the Ku Klux Klan had been organized as a social club in Pulaski, Tennessee. It evolved to an organization dedicated to white supremacy. Dressed in hoods and robes, its members terrorized African Americans in the north and the south, spearheading cross burnings and even murder.

Racism was never confined to southern states. African Americans who migrated north often had a hard time finding a job because of the color of their skin.

Despite all the negatives, the 1870s also offered a rare window of opportunity. Scott Joplin grew up as a member of the first generation of free African Americans. Until the Jim Crow laws of the 1890s restricted their choices, most of them enjoyed unimagined freedom.

In 1870, Congress passed the Fifteenth Amendment, which granted all male citizens the right to vote. Here, black and white voters line up for the first time to vote at a small Alabama town.

Scott did what he could with what he was offered. For him the greatest conflicts took place inside his home. Before he reached adolescence, Giles and Florence split up. His father remarried soon afterward. Although he continued to tell Scott what to do and how to live his life, he provided little financial support for the family. Florence was forced to take in more laundry and clean more houses to feed her children. She also had to move to the less expensive part of Texarkana, in Arkansas.

It was a tough time for Scott. At least his mother's work allowed him to play better instruments. While she cleaned the houses of the wealthy, he practiced on their pianos. Maybe having a chance to touch quality keyboards opened his eyes to the possibilities. Maybe he let himself dream, imagining a larger house and a brand-new piano.

By the time Scott was fourteen, he knew that he wanted to be a professional musician. When he told his father what he wanted to do, Giles was furious. Maybe he was worried his son would starve to death trying to earn a living. Maybe he was just afraid his son would succeed at a career he'd been too scared to pursue. Regardless, when Giles told his son there was an opening at the railroad yard where he worked, he expected Scott to take it.

Scott wasn't interested.

Because schools were segregated—divided by race—Scott couldn't attend the "white" school. In the 1870s Texarkana didn't have schools for African Americans. Instead his family and a few others hired a tutor. Scott did well at his lessons. In fact, the more personal attention probably gave him a better education than he'd have gotten at school. Unfortunately, university educations for African Americans—northern or southern—were still almost nonexistent. Scott knew his future: either playing piano or performing manual labor. It wasn't a tough choice.

By 1882, Scott stopped listening to his father. He preferred to listen to his mother. She always believed in him, always believed he could make a living as a musician. It would dishonor her to do anything other than what he loved.

At about the same age when most kids today are entering high school, Scott Joplin entered a future as uncertain as his father's had been when he was freed from slavery. ◆

RECONSTRUCTION

In 1867, the U.S. Congress passed the Reconstruction Act. It took a hard-line approach to the former Confederate states. More than 200,000 Union soldiers were sent to southern states to enforce the freedom granted to former slaves. Their protection would soon prove very necessary. Some southern veterans were outraged by the new rights given to former slaves, even as they had some of their rights restricted, such as the right to vote.

For the first time African Americans were able to cast ballots in large numbers. For ten years their efforts led to other African Americans' gaining elected office, including two U.S. senators from Mississippi, Hiram Revels and Blanche Bruce. In all, sixteen African Americans reached the U.S. Congress, while some six hundred were elected to southern state legislatures. During the decade, over 4,000 new public schools and nine colleges were opened.

In 1875, Congress passed the landmark Civil Rights Act. It prohibited racial discrimination. African Americans were guaranteed equal access to everything, from movie theaters to jobs.

Unfortunately, the progress of Reconstruction was short-lived. In 1877, U.S. soldiers left the south and the new rights given to former slaves seemed to follow. In 1883, the U.S. Supreme Court declared that the Civil Rights Act was unconstitutional. Soon after the ruling, southern

states began passing Jim Crow laws. These laws required African Americans to use separate (and usually inferior) facilities from whites and applied to everything from bathrooms and water fountains to restaurants and schools. Various voting laws put restrictions on African Americans and made it nearly impossible (and dangerous) for them to vote. It would take almost a century before southern African Americans would regain many of the rights they'd won during Reconstruction.

Scott Joplin composed many of his most famous rags at this piano.

CHAPTER 3

The Piano Man

W hen he was sixteen, Scott formed the Texas Medley Quartette with his brother Will and two neighbors. Soon they added a fifth member, Scott's brother Robert. They traveled wherever they could find work, mostly in eastern Texas and as far north as Missouri.

At some point between the ages of seventeen and twenty, Scott was ready to strike out on his own. Although he'd later tour again with the Texas Medley Quartette, his greatest success would come as a solo act. Getting a gig, a paying job playing music, was easier in the late 1800s than it is now. After all, there was only one kind of music at bars and taverns: live music. The "jukebox" was a piano player and nearly every bar had one. That was how Scott Joplin started earning a living. For several years he traveled among the towns and cities along the Mississippi River, playing in bars and brothels, earning his living at some of the lowest places in nineteenth-century America. By the time he reached St. Louis, Missouri, around 1890, he was used to performing before difficult crowds.

St. Louis was a boomtown. Before the railroads crisscrossed the country, port cities on rivers grew quickly and St. Louis was rightly called the Gateway to the West. Many of the people who stopped there were on their way somewhere else. The travelers' hunger for entertainment fed the city's reputation as a place where anything was available for the right price, most of it near Chestnut Street. The so-called Chestnut Valley boasted numerous bars, hotels, and brothels and provided pianists with steady work.

Scott made his way to the Silver Dollar Saloon, a club owned and operated by an African-American pianist named John Turpin. Turpin helped other musicians find jobs at the local bars and taverns. He earned his nickname "Honest John" by the careful way he treated fellow musicians. He liked Scott's playing so much, he let the twenty-two-year-old work at his own bar, and also helped him find other jobs nearby. When he realized Scott didn't have a place to stay, he invited him to live at his house.

John Philip Sousa (1854-1932) was a bandmaster and composer. Known as the March King, he wrote over 140 marches, many of which are still popular today.

Scott remained for over two years.

Working at bars wasn't an easy way to make a living. Surrounded by drunken, rowdy customers, Scott felt out of place. Some musicians were carousers, but Scott was quiet. He preferred to let his music do the talking for him.

It spoke well.

While Scott was working in bars, the most popular music was the marches of John Philip Sousa. Scott played them in the bars where he worked. After a while he started mixing up the marches with bits of gospel music and classical compositions. Similar to the way some musicians today create new songs from old ones, the "sampling" Scott did was called "ragging." It was enormously popular. It even made bar patrons turn from their drinks or their companions and pay attention to the small, well-dressed man behind the piano.

Classical music is usually smooth and flowing, but the music Scott and his peers created had a syncopated rhythm that seemed choppy or ragged to some listeners. "Ragged time," or "ragtime," music was music you could dance to.

Tom Turpin wanted to put Joplin's music on paper. Joplin turned him down, because he did not believe his music would sell.

Scott used the Turpin home as his base in St. Louis, but he also spent a fair amount of time traveling around Missouri getting jobs in smaller towns. During his second year in St. Louis he met Tom Turpin, John's son, who'd been away working in western mines. Tom was a talented pianist who dreamed of earning a living as a composer. Scott wasn't interested. As far as he was concerned, he was just an African American who played piano in saloons. What music publisher would be interested in him?

Instead, Scott used his talent to travel. In 1893, he left St. Louis for Chicago and looked for work at the World's Columbian Exposition. Although he may not have found much work at the exposition, going to Chicago greatly influenced Scott's life. For the first time he saw African-American musicians treated with respect by white audiences. He realized it was possible for him to make music that wwould be widely accepted.

During his time in Chicago, Scott formed another band with musicians he met there. By 1895 it became a re-formed Texas Medley Quartette. Along with his brothers Will and Robert, and fellow pianist Otis Saunders whom he'd met in Chicago, the group created a "double quartette," with four extra band members and four extra singers. They landed a management company, the Majestic Booking Agency. Over the next two years, they traveled the country, from upstate New York to Oklahoma and Texas.

Scott began composing, after refusing to do so for years. He didn't have a choice. If he wanted the band to play his songs, he'd have to write them down. Once he wrote them down, he figured he might as well see if any music companies were interested in publishing them.

They were. In 1895, he published two songs, "Please Say You Will" and "A Picture of Her Face," which included the opening lines, "This Life is very sad to me, a sorrow fills my heart/My story I will tell you, from me my love did part."[1] Although there is no record of an important woman in Scott's life at this point, the sentimental song suggests that he already knew something about heartbreak.

The next year he sold "Harmony Club Waltz" and "Combination March," which were very similar to the hundreds of pieces of sheet music published that year. "The Crush Collision March" was different. Based on an actual train wreck, it included the noise of the trains hurtling toward each other at sixty miles an hour, followed by a whistle and then the crash of the actual collision.

Although Scott's own life wasn't moving at sixty miles per hour, he was on a collision course with ragtime and a popular club over a feed store. ◆

CHICAGO'S WORLD FAIR

Designed to celebrate the 400th anniversary of Christopher Columbus's voyage to North America, the World's Columbian Exposition was a year late but nobody really complained. Erected on the shores of Lake Michigan, the exhibits and buildings were designed to showcase the best of the United States during the Gilded Age, the period near the end of the nineteenth century. Operating for six months, the fair attracted over 27 million visitors.

Besides Joplin (whose fame would come later), well-known fairgoers included Frederick Douglass, Henry Adams, and Helen Keller, who said, "I took in the glories of the fair with my fingers . . . in the three weeks I spent at the fair I took a long leap from the little child's interest in fairy tales and toys to the appreciation of the real and earnest in the work-a-day world."[2]

An appreciation of the work-a-day world was sorely needed in 1893 as the United States was entering a period of economic depression, when many people lost their jobs. The fair celebrated a kind of utopia, reflecting a positive view of the changes in America as the country moved from rural to urban. The fair's developers envisioned an opportunity for education, allowing attendees to listen to all types of lectures and view cultural exhibits. Most fairgoers weren't interested in that sort of thing. Instead it was the Midway, which featured entertainment such as belly dancers and loud music, that attracted most of them.

The fair would be accused of commercialism, putting money over everything else. The famed writer Leo Tolstoy described it as a place where "Everything is done for profit and amusement—from boredom," even though he never actually went to the fair.[3] The same complaints are still heard today at many similar fairs and exhibitions.

"The Ragtime Dance" was first performed at Wood's Opera House, pictured above, in 1899, in Sedalia, Missouri. Joplin could afford to produce the ballet only once.

CHAPTER
4

Turning Over a New Leaf

S elling his first compositions gave Scott Joplin a new sense of confidence. When the Texas Medley Quartette broke up and its members went their separate ways, Scott wasn't disappointed. He settled in a small town he'd first visited a few years before, a place that would have a greater influence on his music than the big cities of St. Louis or Chicago.

Sedalia, Missouri, was physically less than 200 miles west of St. Louis, but a million miles away in attitude. It had been founded in 1857 by General George R. Smith. He named it after his daughter, Sarah, whose nickname was Sed. He chose its location because it was close to railroads. By the 1890s, seven different railroad lines had junctions in Sedalia. The railroads, and the workers and wages they brought in, made Sedalia prosperous. The town boasted eight hotels, about two dozen restaurants, and over thirty bars. Nearly every one needed a piano player.

Sedalia, like most communities in those days, had a "white" part of town and a "black" part, but both areas were pleasant and well kept. There was much less of the racial tension that Scott had experienced in St. Louis. The comfortable atmosphere brought out his best. He even returned to school, studying at the Smith School of Music, part of a newly opened college for African Americans. Besides attending school, Scott began giving piano lessons for extra money. His students included Arthur Marshall, a teenager whose family ran the boardinghouse where Scott lived, and Scott Hayden.

On January 27, 1897, white bandleader William H. Krell published "Mississippi Rag," the first song with the word rag in the title. It was more of a march than a rag, but just a few months later Scott's old friend Tom Turpin published "Harlem Rag." By then a growing interest in ragtime music was unmistakable. Across the country, all kinds of people, black and white, rich and poor, were doing new dance called the cakewalk. That dance, as well as many others, needed music. Ragtime was perfect.

Scott saw his chance.

Stable employment allowed Scott the free time to pursue his dreams. In 1898 the Maple Leaf Club opened over a feed store at 121 East Main Street. It was a private club for local African Americans, but the audiences were a mixture of all races. Scott landed a gig as the "house man," the club's full-time piano player.

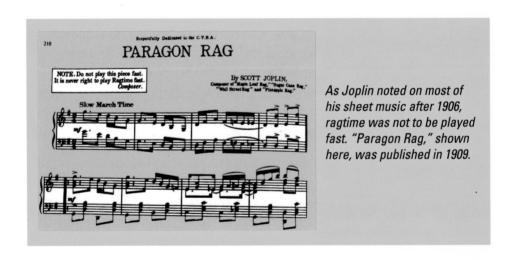

As Joplin noted on most of his sheet music after 1906, ragtime was not to be played fast. "Paragon Rag," shown here, was published in 1909.

Scott's playing was advertised in newspapers and on the club's business cards.

Now that he had a secure job and was not as worried about money, Scott used his free time to write ragtime compositions in earnest. He scribbled notes in quiet moments at the boardinghouse or in a corner of the Maple Leaf Club before the customers arrived.

When he'd finished a few songs, he took them to a local publisher, A. W. Perry and Sons. To them the music seemed unfamiliar. They might have heard of Tom Turpin's rag, but if they had they also knew it had sold only a few hundred copies in St. Louis. They needed a better return for their money. Perry turned Scott down.

Disappointed but hardly willing to give up, Scott made a trip to Kansas City, Missouri, and the Carl Hoffman Music Company. The young composer couldn't get a meeting with Hoffman. Charles Daniels, a composer and arranger who worked for Hoffman, agreed to look at the compositions. Daniels liked what he saw. Hoffman was a bit harder to convince, but agreed finally to publish one of the songs. The result was that in March 1899, Scott's first ragtime song appeared, titled appropriately enough, "Original Rags." It sold modestly, but did well enough for Scott to think he might have a future. Unfortunately, Hoffman wasn't interested in any of his other compositions. These included Scott's "Maple Leaf Rag." As future events would show, that was an enormous error in judgment.

It wasn't long before another man would recognize Scott Joplin's potential. It was a sultry summer that last year of the nineteenth century, and ragtime's popularity was growing. With the help of a young boy and a good song, Scott convinced John Stark to buy "Maple Leaf Rag." Stark was small time, a barely successful Sedalia businessman, but he loved ragtime. He would go to any of the local clubs that played it, even if his was the only white face in the room.

Scott convinced Stark to give him a royalty of a penny per sale. That meant that every copy of the music sold would earn Scott one cent. It was an uncommon arrangement for an unknown composer. Generally music publishers paid a fixed sum of between twenty-five and fifty dollars. Scott was confident about asking for a piece of the action. "Arthur, the 'Maple Leaf' will make me King of Ragtime composers," he'd earlier bragged to his student Arthur Marshall.[1]

John Stark wasn't as confident. He liked the music, but based on the sale of previous ragtime pieces, Stark doubted the one-cent royalty would pay more than a few dollars to Scott. At first it appeared that he was right.

" 'Maple Leaf Rag' was hardly a smash hit at first," says author James Haskins. "As John Stark later said, '. . . it took us one year to sell 400 copies, simply because people examined it hastily, and didn't find it.' "[2] The "it," Haskins believes, was the tune. People either couldn't find it or decided that it was too difficult to play. The result was that Scott earned about four dollars from the first printing.

Things were about to change in a big way. Because of the sudden popularity of dances such as the cakewalk, ragtime music became even more popular and began to sweep the nation. Stark believed that "Maple Leaf Rag" would benefit from this increased interest. He moved to St. Louis and issued a second printing of 10,000 copies.

That printing sold out quickly. So did the third. In fact, "Maple Leaf Rag" has never stopped selling. It would sell one million copies in Scott's lifetime. It would become the world's most popular rag, and it would never go out of print.

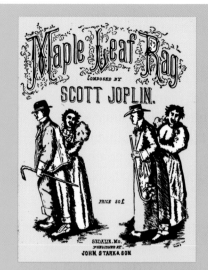

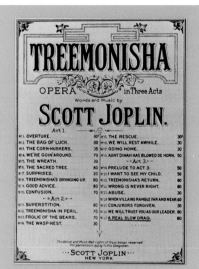

Joplin's "Maple Leaf Rag" was quickly dubbed "King of Rags." His opera Treemonisha, *however, would not see success until the 1970s.*

As author Edward Berlin points out, "There is no question as to the popularity of the 'Maple Leaf Rag.' Everyone interested in piano ragtime played it, or at least tried to play it." Pianist and composer J. Russel Robinson (1892-1963) said, "One of the tunes I played a lot while touring the South was Scott Joplin's 'Maple Leaf Rag.' I think it is one of the finest tunes ever written . . . the King of Rags, and in my way of thinking, nothing that Joplin or any other rag writers wrote ever came close to it."[3]

"Maple Leaf Rag" changed the life of the man who published it and the composer who wrote it.

John Stark decided to devote his business to ragtime. Scott followed his publisher to St. Louis in 1901, but he didn't return to the familiar city alone. He brought with him a new bride, Belle Hayden. She'd married Scott Hayden's brother Joe, but he died leaving her a struggling widow. Scott Hayden and his wife, Nora, joined the Joplins, student and teacher renting a house together with their wives.

Ragtime was huge and growing. St. Louis, with its many ragtime composers and players, along with Tom Turpin's brand-new club The Rosebud, was its center. Although Scott avoided the competitive piano playing that took place there, he enjoyed its atmosphere. In St. Louis, Scott was a hero and a celebrity, an African American who'd risen above his circumstances to write the most popular rag in America.

Despite the popularity of "Maple Leaf Rag," Scott wasn't exactly getting rich off the royalties. He was probably making about the same amount as a factory worker, which provided enough money to cover his living expenses. He decided to devote his time to writing. As far as he was concerned, his days of performing in rowdy, smoke-filled bars were over. He believed ragtime should be as embraced and respected as classical music.

Unfortunately, Scott had a problem with the other composers in ragtime. It wasn't the music, it was the lyrics. Songs that suited the bars and brothels where the music was played were considered vulgar by most members of polite society.

"If someone were to put vulgar words to a strain of one of Beethoven's beautiful symphonies," Scott once said, "people would be saying, 'I don't like Beethoven's symphonies.' "[4]

Scott knew obscene language was ruining ragtime.

He tried to turn the attention of the audiences away from the vulgarity, composing "Swipesy" with his former student Arthur Marshall and "Sunflower Slow Day" with Scott Hayden the next year. He also released his own rag, the more introspective "Peacetime Rag."

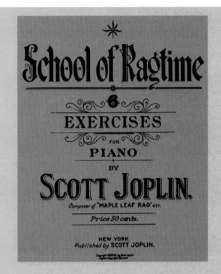

In 1901, Joplin began devoting his time to writing instead of performing. "School of Ragtime" was an exercise book he wrote for his students. "The Chrysanthemum" was published in 1904.

Despite his hard work and ragtime's popularity, a certain segment of the population would never accept ragtime as anything more than "fun music." Educated people didn't seem to like the music. This was especially true of successful African Americans, who were still insecure in their new social status. Even though they may have enjoyed ragtime music, they may have been afraid that expressing that enjoyment would have made them seem low-class.

The result musically was that more and more rags were being written by white composers, who changed it to make it more acceptable to a mass audience. Considering that the best-selling work was created by an African American, this is fairly surprising.

Scott wanted to demonstrate that ragtime could be as versatile as classical, that it could function as music for an opera or a ballet. At Wood's Opera House in Sedalia, he'd conducted a single performance of "The Ragtime Dance." A singing narrator instructed couples as they performed various popular African-

New Orleans became a hotspot for jazz, which Jelly Roll Morton, a popular jazz pianist, claimed he invented by mixing ragtime, blues, and quadrille.

American dances, from the dude walk to the backstep to the show's title number.

In St. Louis, Scott asked John Stark to publish the songbook from the show. It was a huge request; the book was much longer than a normal ragtime song. Stark couldn't imagine anyone buying the book to a show they'd never seen, to perform it in their living room.

Stark refused. The rejection created a rift between them. Although Scott would continue to sell some of his songs through Stark, he'd also sell to other publishers and even self-publish.

By 1903, Scott had problems beyond his career. He and Belle had moved into a huge house on Lucas Street, where they rented out rooms to cover expenses. Belle took care of that, while Scott continued to write. The two spent less and less time together. In 1903 they had a daughter, but she died just a few months after she was born.

The tragedy ended the relationship. When Belle left him, Scott went to his student Hayden and begged the younger man to help him get her back. There was nothing he could do. The marriage was over. Scott Joplin's career began to fade almost as quickly. ◆

THE CAKEWALK

Today when people say, "That takes the cake," they're generally shocked or impressed. But a century ago, when people said those words at a dance competition, someone actually got a cake.

Many organized, almost choreographed, dances became popular in the homes and clubs of the late nineteenth and early twentieth centuries. The cakewalk was probably the most popular. A high-stepping, almost silly dance, it was first done to march music and later to ragtime. Bert Williams and George Walker, two popular black dance performers, often entertained their audience by performing cakewalks to ragtime music.

Bert Williams and George Walker

The dance originated about 1850 in Florida among African-American slaves, who borrowed some of the steps and movements from the local tribe of Seminole Indians. The dance used energetic jumps and twisting movements combined with a promenade—couples walking in a circle, arm in arm. The dance seemed made for ragtime with its fast rhythm and occasionally slower paces. It quickly spread through other areas of the South. Before the Civil War, plantation owners would invite neighbors to watch their slaves have a dance contest. The winners would receive a cake, which is how the dance got its name. After slaves were freed in 1865, its popularity continued. So did the practice of giving prizes.

When whites vacationing in the South in the late nineteenth century returned north, they brought the dance with them. It was the first dance to cross over from black to white society. By 1900 it seemed like everyone was doing it, and the prizes in cakewalk competitions kept getting better. Prizes started as various treats and desserts, especially a cake. Whoever took the cake was expected to share with the other dancers. Soon prizes included jewelry like diamond rings. Fewer winners were inclined to share.

By the 1920s the cakewalk had virtually disappeared. But traces of cakewalk moves remain in such modern dances as the Lindy Hop.

A band plays "Maple Leaf Rag" at Scott Joplin's gravesite. The bronze marker was placed there by members of ASCAP (American Society of Composers, Authors and Publishers) in 1974, fifty-seven years after Joplin's death.

CHAPTER
5

Ragtime Opera

I n the early 1900s, ragtime was huge. Across the United States, in cities like Chicago, Nashville, and New York, composers were writing and musicians were playing the music Scott Joplin first made famous. In 1902, Joplin published "The Entertainer," which would survive the century as his best-known work.

Scott tried to make the most out of the country's taste for ragtime, but he had higher ambitions as well. Despite the title of his new song, he knew the music could do more than just entertain. It could also enlighten. He would spend the last years of his life trying to prove it.

The director of the St. Louis Choral Society, Alfred Ernst, predicted that Scott would soon "do something fine in a composition of a higher class."[1] Ernst was right.

In 1903, Scott toured the Midwest with his ragtime opera, *A Guest of Honor*. The tour was a disaster. Early in its run, the company's treasurer made off with the show's money. Scott was forced to pay everyone himself. With over two dozen singers and musicians, along with hotel and train expenses, the financial burden was huge. The show lost a great deal of money as the performers played to half-empty theaters in places like Fremont, Nebraska, and Mason City, Iowa.

The problem was that opera fans were rarely interested in ragtime, and most ragtime audiences didn't care for opera. In the end, Scott was forced to cancel the last few performances. He moved back to St. Louis and took a room with the Turpins. He arrived just as the city was gearing up for the 1904 World's Fair. While he didn't perform personally, he contributed a rag, "The Cascades." By the time the fair began, Scott's attentions were elsewhere.

In the beginning of the year he traveled to Arkansas to visit relatives. While there he met Freddie Alexander, a nineteen-year-old who'd grown up close to his hometown. The two quickly fell in love and they were married on June 14, 1904. Unfortunately their happiness was short-lived. Freddie caught a cold just after the wedding and spent much of the summer sick in bed. On September 10, she passed away.

Devastated and alone, Scott abandoned Sedalia for St. Louis. By the time he arrived, many of the best-known ragtime performers were leaving for Chicago, where there was more work. His old publisher John Stark left as well, moving to Tin Pan Alley in New York, the center for much of the songwriting and music production in the early twentieth century.

Although Scott tried his luck in Chicago, his heart wasn't in performing. As a composer he found more success in New York, where he relocated in 1907. Although unfamiliar with the city and the ways of selling music there, he found that his name opened doors. Over the next few years he'd sell a number of compositions, including a few to Stark.

Scott also published a three-page book of exercises called "School of Ragtime." In its introduction he wrote, "Syncopations are no indication of light or trashy music. . . . To assist amateur players in giving the 'Joplin rags,' that weird and intoxicating effect intended by the composer, is the object of this work."[2]

He moved away from composing rags as he focused on what he believed would be his greatest work. It was another ragtime opera: *Treemonisha*. At 230 pages, the score was impossible to sell. No publisher would risk printing something so huge.

The opera is about an African-American Arkansas girl given the name Treemonisha by her adoptive family. As Edward Berlin says, "In part, the opera is a tribute to both his mother, for the way that *Treemonisha* obtains her education, and to Freddie, with the opera's action occurring in September 1884, the month and year of Freddie's birth. The opera's story relates how Treemonisha, the only educated member of her community, leads her townspeople out of the bondage of ignorance and superstition."[3] Its lesson, one that Scott actively embraced, was that education was the key to progress in the African-American community. But perhaps that notion was too controversial for the early 1900s.

Scott poured most of his energy into promoting the show. He had the score published at his expense in 1911 and threw parties celebrating it. Soon afterward, he had a piano run-through without costumes and props. Unfortunately few people attended, and none of those who saw the show were interested in funding it.

Scott was crushed. By the time he realized his show would not go on, it was 1913; he was nearly broke. By then he had been married to Lottie Stokes for several years. The couple moved to Harlem in 1914. As was the case with his first marriage, his wife ran their home as a boardinghouse while he wrote. He also set up a mail order business for his sheet music.

Scott's focus was poor. Many years earlier, he had contracted syphilis, a then-untreatable sexually transmitted disease. Its progress was slow, but in the early 1900s it was almost always fatal.

By 1915, when musician Eubie Blake saw Scott perform, the composer was already showing symptoms of decline. "He was so far gone . . . he sounded like a child trying to pick out a tune."[4] Unfortunately, tremors are one of the symptoms of syphilis. Scott couldn't coordinate his fingers. Sadly, the only recorded music we have of Scott's playing dates from this period. None of the recordings give a hint of the talent he once had.

By January 1917, Scott's depression and delusions were too much for Lottie to handle. She had him committed to a mental asylum. On April 1 of that year, Scott Joplin died at Manhattan State Hospital. He was buried in an unmarked grave. In many ways ragtime seemed to die with him. The music gave way to jazz in the 1920s, with its greater emphasis on improvisation.

Fortunately, the United States rediscovered Scott Joplin in the 1970s. The 1973 film *The Sting* helped repopularize music like "The Entertainer." In October 1975, *Treemonisha* finally made its debut on Broadway. The next year, Scott Joplin was awarded a special Bicentennial Pulitzer Prize for the contributions he made to American music.

An honor of a different sort had taken place two years earlier. Members of ASCAP (American Society of Composers, Authors and Publishers) conducted a brief memorial service at his gravesite. A bronze marker labeled simply "Scott Joplin, American composer," and listing his dates of birth and death, was placed on the ground to mark his final resting place.

As James Haskins observes, "During Joplin's lifetime, most of his fellow composers did not recognize his importance; now, at last, they paid him the honor due him. As the dignitaries stood viewing the marker, a soft breeze came up, wafting across the gravesite brightly colored maple leaves from the large tree nearby."[5] ◆

THE STING

It isn't often that a musician who has been dead for half a century makes it onto the pop music charts, but in 1974 that is exactly what happened to Scott Joplin. It was all because of a movie.

The movie was *The Sting*. Released late in 1973, it is set in Chicago in the 1930s and stars two of the top actors of the seventies, Robert Redford and Paul Newman. After a mob boss kills their friend, the Redford and Newman characters decide to get even. They conduct a very elaborate con, or "sting," as their revenge, rather than trying to kill the mob boss. The movie is fast paced and filled with a series of hilarious and often unexpected twists and turns. The film's director, George Roy Hill, needed music that would fit in with the period and with all the lighthearted action.

Robert Redford in
The Sting.

What could be better than ragtime? Hill's son and nephew often played Joplin's rags on the piano at home. Hill quickly realized that Joplin's music would be perfect for the movie. He asked musician/composer Marvin Hamlisch to take on the project. Part of the soundtrack consists of Hamlisch playing Joplin's rags on the piano, while other parts are orchestral arrangements of Joplin's music. The title track features the rag "The Entertainer," and it has become so famous that many people often think of it simply as "The Sting."

The movie's sound track became a top seller as soon as it was released. "The Entertainer" was on the Billboard single charts for twelve weeks. The film won seven Oscars at the 1974 Academy Awards. No one was surprised that one of the Oscars was for the best sound track. A whole new generation had discovered the music of Scott Joplin.

Left to right: Robert Shaw, Robert Redford and Paul Newman in a scene from *The Sting*.

Selected Works

Operas
Treemonisha
A Guest of Honor

Ballet
Ragtime Dance

Piano compositions
A Picture of Her Face
Please Say You Will
The Crush Collision March
Original Rags
Maple Leaf Rag

Swipesy—Cake Walk
Easy Winners
A Breeze from Alabama
Cleopha
The Entertainer
Palm Leaf Rag
Weeping Willow
Cascades
Favorite
Bethena
Rosebud March
Antoinette

Lily Queen
Fig Leaf Rag
Country Club
Paragon Rag
Wall Street Rag
Stoptime Rag
Felicity Rag
Scott Joplin's New
  Rag
Kismet Rag
Magnetic Rag
Reflection Rag

Chronology

1868 Born on November 24 in Bowie County, Texas
1875 Plays the piano for the first time; begins lessons with J. C. Johnson
1880 Takes lessons with Julius Weiss; his parents separate
1884 Forms Texas Melody Quartette
1888 Leaves home to become a professional musician
1890 Reaches St. Louis, Missouri
1893 Moves to Chicago
1895 Tours with Texas Melody Quartette; first two songs are published
1897 Settles in Sedalia, Missouri; begins attending Smith College of Music
1898 Becomes regular pianist at the new Maple Leaf Club
1899 Publishes "Maple Leaf Rag"
1900 Marries Belle Hayden
1901 Returns to St. Louis
1902 Publishes "The Entertainer"
1903 Belle leaves him
1904 Marries Freddie Alexander, but she dies three months after the wedding
1907 Moves to New York
1909 Marries Lottie Stokes
1911 Publishes *Treemonisha*
1917 Admitted to Manhattan State Hospital in New York; dies on April 1
1972 *Treemonisha* is staged at the Atlanta Memorial Arts Center and reaches Broadway three years later
1973 The movie *The Sting* repopularizes Joplin's work
1976 Receives a special Pulitzer Prize in music
1983 U.S. Postal Service issues a stamp in his honor

Timeline in History

1808 After Great Britain prohibits slavery, British warships patrol the coastline of Sierra Leone to curb slave trading.

1820 Under terms of the Missouri Compromise, Missouri is admitted to the Union as a slave state while Maine is admitted as a free state.

1846 Belgian instrument maker Adolphe Sax invents the saxophone.

1857 The Missouri Compromise is ruled unconstitutional by the U.S. Supreme Court during the case of Dred Scott, a slave captured in a free state and forced to return to his owner.

1861 The Civil War begins.

1865 The Civil War ends. The Thirteenth Amendent abolishes slavery.

1868 U.S. President Andrew Johnson is impeached but later acquitted by the Senate. The Fourteenth Amendment grants citizenship to African Americans.

1870 The Fifteenth Amendment grants all male U.S. citizens the right to vote.

1871 France's defeat in the Franco-Prussian War leads to the establishment of the German Empire.

1875 Captain Matthew Webb becomes the first man to swim across the English Channel.

1882 Robert Louis Stevenson publishes his novel *Treasure Island*.

1888 Jack the Ripper murders six women in London, England.

1896 The first modern Olympic Games take place in Athens, Greece.

1903 Henry Ford incorporates the Ford Motor Company in Detroit, Michigan.

1905 Italian operatic composer Giuseppe Verdi dies.

1906 A major earthquake in San Francisco kills over 1,000 people.

1907 French classical composer Claude Debussy writes "Golliwog's Cakewalk," which is greatly influenced by ragtime music.

1912 *Titanic* sinks on her maiden voyage, drowning 1,500 people.

1917 The Russian Revolution begins and leads to the installation of a communist government the following year.

1929 The stock market crash leads to the Great Depression, a period of high unemployment and economic uncertainty in the United States

1941 The Japanese attack on the Pearl Harbor naval base pulls the United States into World War II.

1956 The Birmingham Bus Boycott, an important first step in civil rights for African Americans, begins.

1963 Dr. Martin Luther King, Jr., leads the March on Washington, where he delivers his famous "I have a dream" speech on the steps of the Lincoln Memorial.

1975 U.S. author E. L. Doctorow publishes his novel *Ragtime*.

1998 *Ragtime: The Musical*, based on Doctorow's novel, opens on Broadway and wins four Tony Awards.

Chapter Notes

Chapter 1   Son of a Slave
   1. LeeAnne Gelletly, *Harriet Beecher Stowe* (Philadelphia: Chelsea House Publishers, 2001), p. 42.

Chapter 2   The Struggle After the Freedom
   1. James Haskins, with Kathleen Benson, *Scott Joplin: The Man Who Made Ragtime* (New York: Doubleday and Company, 1978), pp. 43–44.

Chapter 3   The Piano Man
   1. Katherine Preston, *Scott Joplin: Composer* (New York: Chelsea House Publishers, 1988), p. 42.
   2. "World's Columbian Exposition: Idea, Experience, Aftermath," August 1, 1996, http://xroads.virginia.edu/~MA96/WCE/title.html
   3. Ibid.

Chapter 4   Turning Over a New Leaf
   1. Edward A. Berlin, *King of Ragtime: Scott Joplin and His Era* (New York: Oxford University Press, 1994), p. 52.
   2. James Haskins, with Kathleen Benson, *Scott Joplin: The Man Who Made Ragtime* (New York: Doubleday and Company, 1978), p. 102.
   3. Berlin, *King of Ragtime*, p. 56.
   4. Katherine Preston, *Scott Joplin: Composer* (New York: Chelsea House Publishers, 1988), p. 17.

Chapter 5   Ragtime Opera
   1. David A. Jasen and Gene Jones, *Black Bottom Stomp: Eight Masters of Ragtime and Early Jazz* (New York: Routledge, 2002), p. 21.
   2. Ibid., p. 26.
   3. Edward Berlin, "A Biography of Scott Joplin (c. 1867–1917)," Scott Joplin International Ragtime Foundation, http://www.scottjoplin.org/biography.htm.
   4. Jasen and Jones, *Black Bottom Stomp*, p. 29.
   5. James Haskins, with Kathleen Benson, *Scott Joplin: The Man Who Made Ragtime* (New York: Doubleday and Company, 1978), p. 17.

For Further Reading

For Young Adults

Gelletly, LeeAnne. *Harriet Beecher Stowe*. Philadelphia: Chelsea House Publishers, 2001.

Hakim, Joy. *Reconstruction and Reform: 1865-1870*. New York: Oxford University Press, 1999.

Mour, Stanley I. *American Jazz Masters*. Berkeley Heights, N.J.: Enslow Publishers, Inc., 1998.

Otfinoski, Steven. *Scott Joplin: A Life in Ragtime*. New York: Franklin Watts, 1995.

Preston, Katherine. *Scott Joplin: Composer*. New York: Chelsea House Publishers, 1988.

Works Consulted

Berlin, Edward A. *King of Ragtime: Scott Joplin and His Era*. New York: Oxford University Press, 1994.

Gammond, Peter. *Scott Joplin and the Ragtime Era*. New York: St. Martin's Press 1975.

Haskins, James, with Kathleen Benson. *Scott Joplin: The Man Who Made Ragtime*. New York: Doubleday and Company, 1978.

Hasse, John Edward, ed. *Ragtime: Its History, Composers and Music*. New York: Macmillan, 1985.

Jasen, David A., and Gene Jones. *Black Bottom Stomp: Eight Masters of Ragtime and Early Jazz*. New York: Routledge, 2002.

Jasen, David A., and Trebor Jay Tichenor. *Rags and Ragtime: A Musical History*. New York: The Seabury Press, 1978.

On the Internet

The Life of Scott Joplin
http://www.personal.psu.edu/users/j/n/jnm144/scott%20joplin.htm

St. Louis Walk of Fame—Scott Joplin
http://www.stlouiswalkoffame.org/inductees/scott-joplin.html

Scott Joplin—Father of Ragtime Music
http://library.thinkquest.org/10320/Joplin.htm?tqskip1=1&tqtime=0109

Handbook of Texas Online: Joplin, Scott
http://www.tsha.utexas.edu/handbook/online/articles/print/JJ/fjo70.html

World's Columbian Exposition: Idea, Experience, Aftermath
http://xroads.virginia.edu/-MA96/WCE/title.html

The Scott Joplin International Ragtime Foundation
http://www.scottjoplin.org/

Friends of Scott Joplin
http://stlouis.missouri.org/501c/fsjoplin/

Classical Net—Basic Repertoire Net—Joplin
http://www.classical.net/music/comp.lst/joplin.html

Street Swing's Dance History Archives—The Cakewalk History Page
http://www.streetswing.com/histmain/z3cake1.htm

100 Years of the Maple Leaf Rag
http://music.mpr.org/features/9905_ragtime/index.shtml

Index